Dr. Mae Jemison and 100 Year Starship™

Exploring Our Sun

DR. MAE JEMISON
AND DANA MEACHEN RAU

Children's Press®
An Imprint of Scholastic Inc.
New York Toronto London Auckland Sydney
Mexico City New Delhi Hong Kong
Danbury, Connecticut

Library of Congress Cataloging-in-Publication Data

Jemison, Mae, 1956–
  Exploring our sun/by Mae Jemison and Dana Meachen Rau.
      p. cm.—(A true book)
  Includes bibliographical references and index.
  ISBN 978-0-531-25502-5 (library binding) — ISBN 978-0-531-24062-5 (pbk.)
  1. Sun—Juvenile literature. I. Rau, Dana Meachen, 1971– II. Title. III. Series: True book.
  QB521.5.J46 2013
  523.7—dc23   2012035788

© 2013 Scholastic Inc.

All rights reserved. Published in 2013 by Children's Press, an imprint of Scholastic Inc.
Printed in China 62
SCHOLASTIC, CHILDREN'S PRESS, A TRUE BOOK™, and associated logos are trademarks and/or registered trademarks of Scholastic Inc.
4 5 6 7 8 9 10 R 22 21 20 19 18 17 16 15

**Front cover: *Solar Orbiter*
probe near the sun**

**Back cover: Diagram of the
sun's layers**

Find the Truth!

Everything you are about to read is true *except* for one of the sentences on this page.

Which one is **TRUE**?

T or F No other stars give out as much light as the sun.

T or F Our sun is a middle-size star about halfway through its life.

Find the answers in this book.

Contents

1 The Sun Is a Star

What is a star? 7

2 The Life of Stars

How did the solar system form? 13

3 A Power Plant

How does the sun make light? 23

THE **BIG** TRUTH!

Studying the Sun from Space

What have probes taught us about the sun? 28

The sun's energy can create colorful displays in Earth's skies.

4 A Ball of Energy

How does energy travel from the sun to Earth? . . . **31**

5 Thanks to the Sun

Why do we need the sun? **39**

True Statistics **44**

Resources **45**

Important Words **46**

Index **47**

About the Authors **48**

The sun's active surface includes bursts of energy called solar flares.

When a person's surroundings on Earth are dark enough, the Milky Way can be seen in the sky.

CHAPTER 1

The Sun Is a Star

Since the beginning of human history, people have watched a display of twinkling lights in the night sky. They imagined these lights formed pictures, which they called constellations. They used these lights to help **navigate** from one place to another. During the day, people relied on the light and heat from the big, bright ball in the sky. Both these nighttime lights and the daytime sun are stars.

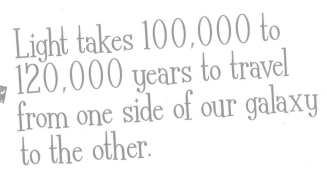

Light takes 100,000 to 120,000 years to travel from one side of our galaxy to the other.

What Is a Star?

A star is an enormous ball of very hot gases. Most of these gases are the elements hydrogen and helium. Hydrogen is the fuel for the star. As the star uses this fuel, it makes energy in the form of light and heat. It also turns the hydrogen into helium.

Stars, including our sun, shine because of the energy produced by the process of turning hydrogen into helium.

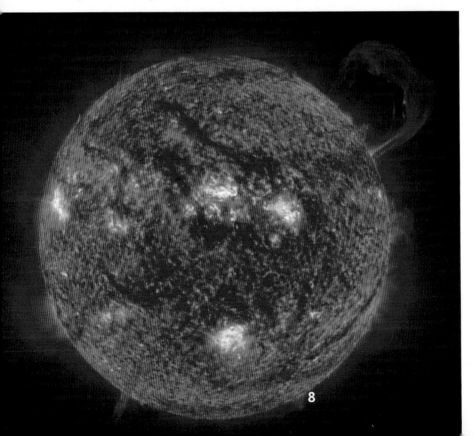

It takes the sun about 200 million years to orbit around the center of the Milky Way galaxy.

The Milky Way appears as a bright band of stars across the night sky.

A galaxy is a group of stars. Galaxies can contain hundreds of billions of stars. Our sun, most of the stars we can see, and many more we can't see are all a part of our galaxy. We call our galaxy the Milky Way. It got this name because there is a band of stars in the middle so **dense** that people thought it looked like spilled milk. There are billions more galaxies in our universe.

Zeta Ophiuchi, shown here surrounded by red dust and gases, is a massive blue star.

Characteristics of Stars

Our sun gives off a lot of light. But some stars in the Milky Way give off 100,000 times more light. How bright a star looks in the sky is its **magnitude**. The temperature of a star determines its color. Blue stars are the hottest. Red are the coolest. Yellow stars are in between. Scientists also look at a star's size. Dwarfs are some of the smallest stars. Supergiants are some of the largest.

The Size of the Sun

Compared to the planets, stars are generally very big. About 1.3 million Earths could fit inside the sun. The sun also has a lot more mass than any of the planets.

Compared to other stars, our sun is a middle-size star. Its distance from center to surface is 432,000 miles (695,237 kilometers). Proxima Centauri, a red dwarf star, is about seven times smaller than the sun. Rigel, a blue supergiant, is almost 80 times larger.

Blue giant Sirius A is much larger than our yellow sun. Proxima Centauri is much smaller.

Proxima Centauri is the closest star to our sun.

Our solar system includes eight planets.
Pluto, the outer-most object in this
diagram, is called a dwarf planet.

CHAPTER 2

The Life of Stars

The sun is the center of our solar system. The solar system includes the eight planets (Mercury, Venus, Earth, Mars, Jupiter, Saturn, Uranus, and Neptune), smaller dwarf planets such as Pluto, asteroids, and comets. The gravity of the sun holds the solar system together. All of these objects orbit in paths around our central star.

Planets closest to the sun orbit faster than those orbiting farther away.

Big Bang

Scientists believe that the entire universe started with a giant explosion. This explosion is often called the Big Bang. Before the Big Bang, one tiny particle contained all the matter and energy that would become all of the galaxies, stars, and planets of the universe.

This diagram shows the development of the universe from a single particle (left) to a collection of galaxies, stars, planets, and other objects.

As the universe expanded, hydrogen collected in clouds.

When this particle exploded, the matter and energy shot out in all directions. The universe spread out. As it did, the gas hydrogen was formed. Hydrogen grouped together into large clouds scattered across the universe. Over time, these clouds would become galaxies.

Stars that are part of a pair orbit around a central point together.

The Start of Our Solar System

Our solar system started to form when a smaller cloud of gas and dust formed within a galaxy. As the cloud grew, it spun. It pulled in more matter. The middle of the cloud became dense. As gases got denser, they had more gravity. Gravity pulled in even more matter. This caused the cloud to spin even faster.

The center of the cloud became so dense that the atoms of hydrogen collided together. The collisions gave off heat. This center of the cloud became our sun. A flat disk of matter continued to spin around the sun. Much of the matter in the outer disk clustered together to make planets. Extra matter became comets and asteroids.

Dust and gas left over from the formation of a star can become planets and other objects.

Life Cycle of Stars

All stars are born, grow, and die. New stars are still being created in clouds called **nebulae**. Our sun was born about 4.6 billion years ago. It is using its fuel to create light and heat energy. It is about halfway through its life. That means it has used up about half of its fuel.

New stars shine through the dust and gas of the Eagle Nebula.

Larger stars have shorter lives than smaller stars.

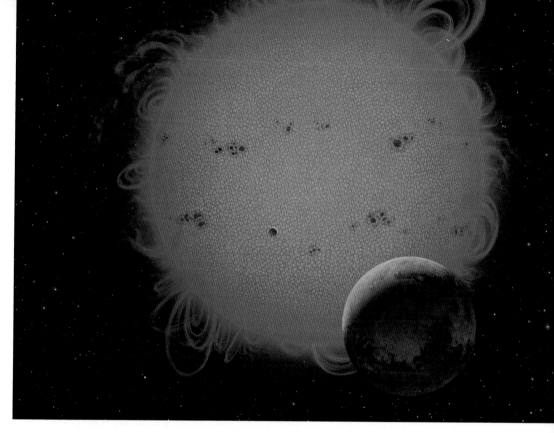

Our sun will eventually become a red giant.

When a star uses up all its fuel, its center, or core, becomes very dense. Gravity pulls in on the star, and it becomes denser and hotter. But as the gases in the star's outer shell get hotter, they push outward, and the star expands. It grows in size. This is called the red giant phase of a star's cycle because of the star's size, brightness, and red color.

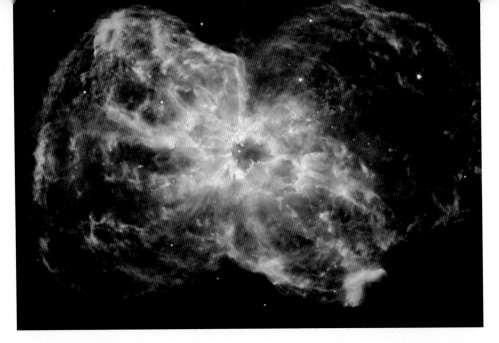

It takes millions of years for a star to develop from a red giant into a white dwarf.

After the red giant phase, the center of the star becomes so dense that its gravity makes the star shrink. Again, the star becomes hotter and the outer gases expand. The star grows bigger and brighter. However, as the gases move away from the core, the pull of gravity becomes weaker. The outer layers drift away. When only the core is left, the star is called a white dwarf. It has little fuel left. Once it cools, it is called a black dwarf.

Heavy Metals

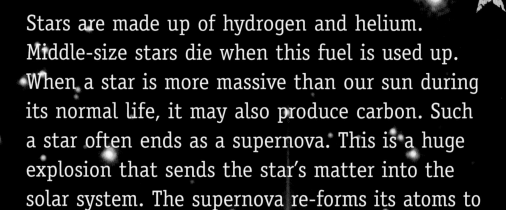

Stars are made up of hydrogen and helium. Middle-size stars die when this fuel is used up. When a star is more massive than our sun during its normal life, it may also produce carbon. Such a star often ends as a supernova. This is a huge explosion that sends the star's matter into the solar system. The supernova re-forms its atoms to create new elements, such as the metals iron and lead, which exist throughout our solar system.

Fusion bombs, sometimes called hydrogen or thermonuclear bombs, use the same process of nuclear fusion as the sun.

CHAPTER 3

A Power Plant

The sun is a giant power plant. Inside, the sun's hydrogen atoms **fuse** together to create helium. This process is called nuclear fusion. The sun creates huge amounts of heat and light energy through nuclear fusion. It is a process that is much more powerful than a nuclear bomb.

Atoms are the tiniest forms of matter.

Making Energy

Energy is created deep in the center of the sun, in its core. The temperature here is 27 million degrees Fahrenheit (15 million degrees Celsius). The core of the sun is very dense gas. The atoms are packed so close together that a piece of the sun the size of a marble would be 10 times heavier than a marble made of lead!

The sun has many layers.

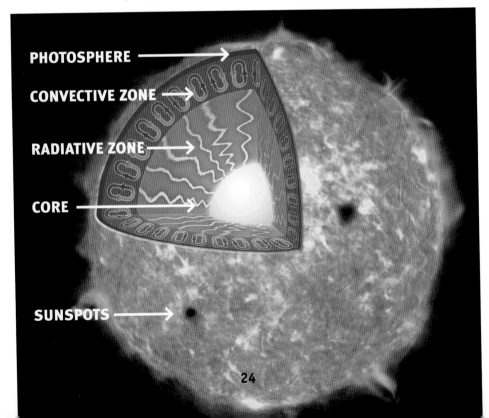

PHOTOSPHERE

CONVECTIVE ZONE

RADIATIVE ZONE

CORE

SUNSPOTS

Energy in the sun moves from the core out to the sun's surface.

The process of turning hydrogen into helium creates energy. This energy moves out from the sun's core toward its surface. First, the energy passes through an area surrounding the core called the radiative zone. This can take more than 100,000 years. Next, the energy passes through the hot and bubbly convective zone. Then it finally reaches the surface.

The photosphere is about the same temperature as Earth's core.

We can see the light of the photosphere from Earth.

At the Surface

The sun's surface is called the photosphere. When the energy reaches the photosphere, it is released into space. The temperature of the photosphere is about 10,000°F (5,538°C). It's a lot cooler than the core. But it is still very hot! The light we see from Earth comes from the photosphere.

The next two layers make up the sun's **atmosphere**. They are called the chromosphere and the corona. We can't really see these layers from Earth, except during a solar eclipse. This is when the Earth, sun, and moon are lined up. The moon blocks the photosphere's light. During an eclipse, the chromosphere appears as a red rim. The corona looks like a fuzzy crown of light around the sun.

The sun's corona can easily be seen during a total eclipse.

Studying the Sun from Space

Scientists on Earth can observe the sun through special telescopes. But to get a closer view, the National Aeronautics and Space Administration (NASA) has sent **probes** on missions to the sun.

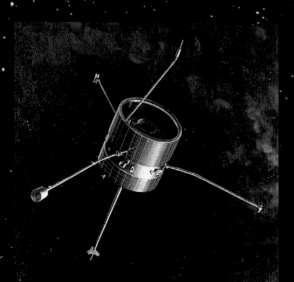

Pioneer 6, 7, 8, and *9* were launched from 1965 to 1968. These probes orbited the sun from four different positions. They acted as weather stations to help scientists predict solar storms.

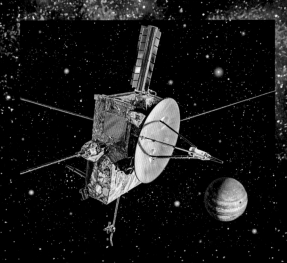

Ulysses, launched in 1990, orbited the sun from top to bottom. This gave scientists a view of the sun's poles. *Ulysses* studied solar storms and solar wind. It studied the sun's magnetic field and its rays.

Genesis, launched in 2001, captured particles from the solar wind. Solar wind is a constant stream of particles sent into space by the sun. *Genesis* returned these particles to Earth three years later for scientists to study.

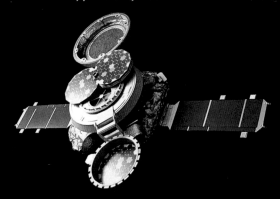

The Solar Probe program is a series of missions. The series started in 2010 and will continue well into the future. It will solve unanswered questions about the sun's corona and solar wind.

When light travels
through moisture in
the air, it separates
into all the colors of
the rainbow.

CHAPTER 4

A Ball of Energy

The energy the sun releases is called radiation. This radiation travels in waves. It takes many forms, such as radio waves and x-rays. The sun's x-rays are the same type of radiation doctors use to see inside our bodies. The sun's radiation also takes the form of the light we can see, called visible light. Visible light appears to be white. But it is actually made up of all the colors of the rainbow.

 Light travels in the form of waves. Red wavelengths are the longest. Violet are the shortest.

Energy to Earth

The energy from the sun travels at the speed of light. The speed of light is 186,282 miles (299,792 km) per second. At this speed, it takes eight minutes for that energy to travel from the sun to Earth. Only about 40 percent of the energy that reaches Earth makes it to Earth's surface. The rest is **absorbed** by Earth's atmosphere or is **reflected** back into space.

Sun Observation Timeline

2000 BCE
Babylonians use sundials to mark time during the day.

800 BCE
Chinese astronomers make the first written record of sunspots.

350 BCE
Aristotle explains that the planets and stars, including the sun, orbit Earth.

300 BCE
Aristarchus of Samos first proposes that Earth orbits the sun.

32

Some of the sun's energy is harmful. Our atmosphere helps protect us by blocking out most of the harmful rays. This includes ultraviolet rays, which cause sunburn and, in extreme cases, cancer. Each minute, enough sunlight reaches Earth's surface to meet the world's energy needs for an entire year!

1543 CE
Nicolaus Copernicus again proposes a sun-centered system.

1610
Through early telescopes, astronomers can observe the sun more closely than ever before.

1962
McMath-Pierce Solar Telescope in Arizona is built to observe the sun with powerful telescopes.

2004
The space probe *Genesis* returns to Earth with samples of particles from solar wind.

Solar Wind

The sun's corona extends millions of miles to the edge of our solar system, past Pluto. It is the source of the solar wind. The solar wind is the stream of particles constantly flowing out from the sun. These particles travel about 250 miles per second (402 km/sec). The particles are magnetic and charged with electricity.

Earth's magnetic field protects the planet from the sun's usual solar wind.

The gases around the sun's poles rotate slower than those at the sun's equator.

When a solar storm is strong enough, it can damage our power grids and even cause blackouts.

Solar Storms

Solar storms are huge bursts of energy from the sun's surface. These can cause problems for people on Earth. Earth is surrounded by a magnetic field. If charged particles from the sun come in contact with that field, this can cause electrical damage. The power grids that provide us electricity might shut down. A solar storm can affect radio signals that help us communicate with airplanes and satellites.

Solar flares shoot bursts of energy and particles into space.

An Active Surface

A solar flare is a sudden increase of brightness and energy coming from the surface of the sun. It happens when energy builds up in the sun's atmosphere. The sun releases the energy in a short burst. A solar flare may only last a few minutes.

Sunspots are areas of the surface that are cooler than other areas. Sunspots grow and shrink. They appear and disappear in cycles over time.

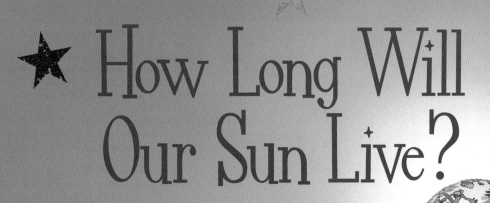

How Long Will Our Sun Live?

Scientists believe that our sun has enough fuel to last about five billion more years. Then it will start to grow into a red giant. It will take about 100 million years to turn into a white dwarf. Then it will take another few billion years for it to cool into a black dwarf.

Our sun will die someday. But you don't have to worry about living without it. Five billion years is a long time!

Earth is located just the right distance from the sun to support life.

CHAPTER 5

Thanks to the Sun

Life on Earth would be impossible without the sun. We are the perfect distance from the sun to benefit from its heat and light. Plants absorb the sun's energy and combine it with liquid water to make food. When we eat plants, we are using the sun's energy, too. That's how we grow and survive. The other planets are either too close to the sun or too far away to support the type of life found on Earth.

Plants give off oxygen, a gas people need to survive.

Effects on the Earth

Earth rotates once every 24 hours. The part of Earth that is facing the sun is constantly changing. It is day on the part facing the sun. Night is on the side facing away. Seasons change as Earth orbits the sun. Sometimes the northern half, or hemisphere, is tilted toward the sun. Then it is summer in North America and other areas in that hemisphere. When the southern hemisphere is tilted closer, it is winter in North America.

Earth's slight tilt causes the northern hemisphere to be closer to the sun during the summer and farther away during winter.

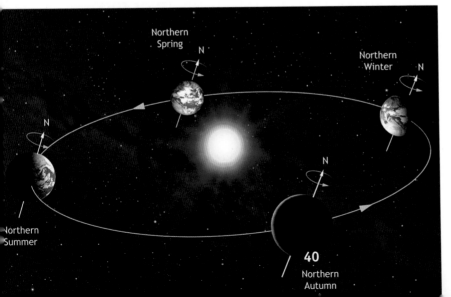

Northern Spring

N

Northern Winter

N

N

N

Northern Summer

40

Northern Autumn

Earth takes 365 days to orbit the sun.

The northern and southern lights are the product of particles from the sun hitting Earth's atmosphere.

Earth's **equator** is always close to the sun, so it has a warmer **climate**. Earth's North and South Poles are always farther from the sun and have a colder climate.

The charged particles carried by the solar wind cause the northern and southern lights. These colorful sky displays can be seen close to Earth's poles. Large bursts of charged particles from solar flares can cause communication problems with radio signals and satellites orbiting Earth.

Solving Mysteries

NASA has sent many missions to the sun, such as *Pioneer*, *Ulysses*, and *Genesis*, to study our closest star. Even though we have learned a lot about it, the sun still holds many mysteries. For example, the photosphere is the closest layer to the core, but the corona is much hotter. Scientists have always wondered why this is true. They have also wanted to know how the solar wind speeds up as it leaves the sun.

Workers check *Genesis* before it is loaded onto a rocket and launched into space in 2001.

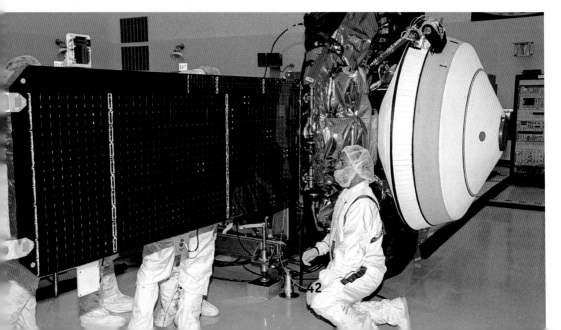

Earth is an average of 93 million miles (150 km) from the sun.

Scientists still have many unanswered questions about the sun.

The Solar Probe program began in 2010. The program involves using spacecraft to gather information. Scientists are designing new spacecraft to get close to the sun where the solar wind begins. They hope the information and images these spacecraft collect will answer their questions about the star that sustains life on Earth. ⭐

Number of Earths that could fit inside the sun: About 1.3 million

The sun's radius (center to surface): 432,000 mi. (695,237 km)

The sun's circumference (distance around) at the equator: 2,715,400 mi. (4,370,000 km)

Age of the sun: 4.6 billion years

Temperature of sun's core: 27,000,000°F (15,000,000°C)

Temperature of the sun's photosphere: 10,000°F (5,538°C)

Time for sun's energy to reach Earth: 8 minutes

Average distance between Earth and the sun: 92.96 million mi. (149.60 million km)

Did you find the truth?

F No other stars give out as much light as the sun.

T Our sun is a middle-size star about halfway through its life.

Resources

Books

Owens, L. L. *The Sun*. Mankato, MN: Child's World, 2010.

Reilly, Carmel. *The Sun*. New York: Marshall Cavendish Benchmark, 2012.

Sparrow, Giles. *The Sun and Stars*. Mankato, MN: Smart Apple Media, 2012.

Than, Ker. *Stars*. New York: Children's Press, 2010.

Waxman, Laura Hamilton. *The Sun*. Minneapolis: Lerner Publications Co., 2010.

Visit the 100 Year Starship Web site at *100YSS.org* for more information on the challenges of travel to another star and ideas on how to solve them. You can also learn about the people who are trying to make the dream a reality!

Visit this Scholastic Web site for more information on exploring our sun:
★ www.factsfornow.scholastic.com
Enter the keywords **Exploring Our Sun**

Important Words

absorbed (ab-ZORBD) — soaked up

atmosphere (AT-muhs-feer) — the mixture of gases that surrounds a planet

climate (KLYE-mit) — the weather typical of a place over a long period of time

dense (DENS) — having a large amount of matter packed tightly together

equator (i-KWAY-tur) — an imaginary line around the middle of a star or planet that is an equal distance from the object's North and South Poles

fuse (FYOOZ) — to combine two pieces of something together by heating them

magnitude (MAG-ni-tood) — the brightness of a star as seen from Earth

navigate (NAV-i-gate) — to find where you are and where you need to go when you travel in a ship, an aircraft, or other vehicle

nebulae (NEB-yuh-lee) — bright areas made of stars or gas and dust

probes (PROHBZ) — a device used to explore space

reflected (ri-FLEKT-id) — threw back heat, light, or sound from a surface

Index

Page numbers in **bold** indicate illustrations.

atmosphere, 27, 32–33, 36, **41**
atoms, 17, 21, 23, 24

Big Bang, **14**–15
brightness. *See* magnitude.

chromosphere, 27
colors, **10**, **11**, **19**, **20**, **30**, 31, 37, **41**
convective zone, **24**, 25
core, 19, 20, **24**, **25**, 26, 42
corona, **27**, 29, 34, 42

density, 9, 16, 17, 19, 20, 24
distance, **38**, 39, 43
dwarf planets, **12**, 13
dwarf stars, 10, **11**, **20**, 37

Earth, 13, **26**, 27, 28, 29, 32, **33**, **34**, 35,
  38, 39, **40–41**, **43**
eclipses, **27**
energy, **8**, 14, 15, 18, 23, 24–**25**, 26, 31,
  32–33, 35, **36**, 39

fuel, 8, 18–19, 20, 21, 37
fusion. *See* nuclear fusion.

galaxies, **6**, 7, **9**, **14**, 15, 16
gases, 8, **10**, **15**, 16, **17**, **18**, 19, 20, 24, 34, 39
gravity, 13, 16, 19, 20

heat. *See* temperatures.
helium, **8**, 21, 23, 25
hydrogen, **8**, **15**, 17, 21, **22**, 23, 25

life, **38**, 39
life cycle, 18–20, 21, 37

light, 7, **8**, 10, 18, 23, **26**, 27, **30**, 31, 32,
  33, 39, **41**

magnetic field, 29, **34**, 35
magnitude, 10, 19, 20, 36
Milky Way galaxy, **6**, **9**, 10

navigation, 7
nebulae, **18**
nuclear fusion, **22**, 23

orbit, 9, 13, **16**, 32, **40**

particles, **14**, 15, 29, **33**, 34, 35, **36**, **41**
photosphere, **24**, **25**, **26**, 27, 42
planets, 11, **12**, 13, **14**, **17**, **34**, 39
poles, 29, 34, 41

radiative zone, **24**, 25

seasons, **40**
sizes, 10, 11, 19, 20, 21
solar flares, **36**, 41
solar storms, 28, 29, **35**
solar system, **12**, 13, 16–17, 21, 34
solar wind, 29, **33**, **34**, 41, 42, 43
space probes, **28–29**, **33**, **42**, 43
sunspots, **24**, 32, 36
supergiants, 10, **11**
supernovas, **21**

temperatures, 7, 8, 10, 17, 18, 19, 20, 23,
  24, 26, 37, 39
timeline, **32–33**

universe, 9, **14**, **15**

About the Authors

Dr. Mae Jemison is leading 100 Year Starship (100YSS). This is a new initiative to make human space travel to another star possible within the next 100 years. Dr. J is a medical doctor, engineer, and entrepreneur, or businessperson. She was a NASA astronaut and flew aboard the space shuttle *Endeavour* in 1992. She was the world's first woman of color in space. Dr. J was a college professor, author, and started several businesses. She also works to get more students involved in science. She started an international science camp for students called The Earth We Share. Dr. J enjoys dancing, gardening, and art. She lives in Houston and loves cats!

Dana Meachen Rau is the author of more than 300 books for children. A graduate of Trinity College in Hartford, Connecticut, she has written fiction and nonfiction titles, including early readers and books on science, history, cooking, and many other topics that interest her. Dana lives with her family in Burlington, Connecticut.